how i
got
ovah

ANCHOR·PRESS·
DOUBLEDAY·

CAROLYN M. RODGERS was born and raised in Chicago, where she now resides. Her poetry has been published in numerous magazines and journals, including *Black World, Ebony, Journal of Black Poetry, Colloquy, The Nation,* and *Essence.* Previous publications include two volumes of poetry, *Paper Soul, Songs of a Blackbird,* and several broadsides. She was a founding member of OBAC (Organization of Black American Culture) and the Gwendolyn Brooks Writing Workshop. Her awards include the first Conrad Kent Rivers Writing Award, a National Endowment for the Arts Award, and the Society of Midland Authors Award.

how i
got
ovah

New and Selected Poems
by Carolyn M. Rodgers

Anchor Books
Anchor Press/Doubleday
Garden City, New York
1976

Library of Congress Cataloging in Publication Data

Rodgers, Carolyn M.
    How i got ovah

    I. Title.
PS3568.0347H6   811'.5'4
ISBN 0-385-04673-1

The Hardcover edition of this book was published
by Doubleday & Company, Inc., 1975.
Anchor Books Edition: 1976

Copyright © 1968, 1969, 1970, 1971, 1972, 1973, 1975 by Carolyn M. Rodgers
Foreword copyright © 1975 by Angela Jackson
All Rights Reserved
Printed in the United States of America

Some of these poems first appeared in publications: "For Our Fathers," *Ebony*,
August 1972 © Johnson Publishing Co.; "Some Body Call (for help)," "Un-
titled (off the track/i blew)," *Jump Bad Anthology*, Broadside Press 1971;
"47th & Vincennes/Chicago," "for sapphires," "Portrait," *Spectrum In Black*,
Scott Foresman 1971; "to Gwen," *To Gwen with Love* © Johnson Publishing
Company 1972; "c. c. rider," *Natural Process*, Hill & Wang 1970; "The Chil-
dren of Their Sin," *Black World*, November 1972; "how i got ovah," *Black
World*, June 1973; "For Some Black Men," "Love—The Beginning and The
End," *Paper Soul*, Third World Press 1968; "For H. W. Fuller," "U Name
This One," "JESUS WAS CRUCIFIED/or It Must Be Deep," "It Is Deep,"
"No Such Thing As A Witch," "BREAKTHROUGH," *Songs of a Black Bird*,
Third World Press 1969.

Dedicated to the Memory
of Bobby and Gregory Rodgers

Contents

carolyn.
singer of sass and blues. has come again.
the skinny knock-kneed little mama of "paper soul"
the pain-struck girl of "songs of a black bird"
has been transformed.
she is all grown up now. boldly beautiful
"blues gettin up" has got up and went. carolyn taken us
some where.
listen at her sanctified soul.
make u testify to truth.

her name is sister. she is yours.
everytime you look at her u see somebody u know.
she remind u of the church.
her eye is seeing holy. she remind u of the people on the corner
                    her words be leaning on the buildings there.
she you sister. she everywhere.
carolyn can do the happy in the aisles of yo mind.
she so country and street and proper too.
she africa and greenville. monroe and pinebluff. chicagonewyorkphilly
l.a. boston batonrouge neworleans atlanta macon and alligator too.
carolyn say "the blues got class." she the blues and something else
everything too.
carolyn is a poet. a downhome choir in herself.
she a witness. will glorify u.
                    will embarrass the ugly.
tell u bout yoself.
she a witness. humming her people
                to the promise/d land.

ANGELA JACKSON
November 1974

Author's Note

When a book is finally published, an author is very likely to have changed his style and his mind. About many things. Most of us writers have to wait quite a while to see ourselves materialize in print, even after we're accepted for publication.

Still, a person does not wish to offer apologies for where she or he was. For certainly where one has been makes where one is more meaningful. Many of you will recognize some of these poems. You will not recognize quite a few others. Some might wonder why I didn't include various old favorites. I simply rejected old favorites because they are just that. Old. And favorite and can be found in practically every anthology I'm in.

I want my work to interest as many people as possible; therefore, some words have been either altered or eliminated completely.

The poems are not placed in any chronological order because I often forget to date my work. Rather, the order is one of sense, touch, and feeling.

CAROLYN M. RODGERS
August, 1974

how i
got
ovah

for muh' dear

today Blackness
lay backin
& rootin

told my sweet mama
to leave me alone
about my wild free knotty and nappy
hair
cause i was gon lay back
and let it grow so high
it could reroute its roots
and highjack the sky!

she sd. why don't you let it grow
right on down to the ground honey chile,
grow yo'self a coat of hair fuh winter
matter fact you so BLACK now, huh!
why don't you jest throw
a fit
of BLACK lay backin & rootin.

my mama gives some boss advice . . .
i think we all ought to do that

The revolution is dead said little willie to joe

just like a balloon thats been flying high the revolution's
gone and lost all its air and fell on the ground
Folks done stomped   it so its almost buried in the dirt

I tell you, Joe, little Willie said,
Black is as tired as it is beautiful.

The "revolutionaries" is whispering so low
you cant git over   or   under em
Looks like to me the women, pimps and dope fiends
is gon run it
I tell you, the revolution is dead, my man, dead.

    Naw, said Joe the revolution aint dead
Sometimes when you be flying in the sky in them airplanes,
you move so fast dont seem like you be moving at all/
And you go up and down hitting air pockets, you dig?
You be hitting hard like a boxer
like a heavyweight boxer that the wite folks got in
    a monkey ring
boxing wid a different person every hour of the day
now you'd be tired, Little Willie if they had you in that bag,
    wouldnt you?
You'd have to either stop fighting altogether, or ease up
    change or tighten your strategy or you'd fall out from

    pure exhaustion.

Naw Little Willie, Joe said
I looks at it this way, my man . . .
    the Revolution aint dead
  its tired,
        and jest resting.

1.15.72

i have changed
so much
in this world
        i am
constantly amazed
to find
the world has
changed
so little,
        and yet
            i have changed
            so little
                i am
            constantly amazed
            to find that
            the world has
            changed
            at all.

i can tell you
about them
i have shaken rivers
out of my eyes
i have waded eyelash deep
have crossed rivers
have shaken the water weed out
of my lungs
have swam for strength
pulled by strength
through waterfalls with electric beats
i have bore the shocks
of water deep deep
waterlogs are my bones
i have shaken the water free of my hair
have kneeled on the banks
and kissed my ancestors of the dirt
whose rich dark root fingers rose up reached out
grabbed and pulled me rocked me cupped me
gentle strong and firm
carried me
made me swim for strength
cross rivers
though i shivered
was wet was cold
and wanted to sink down
and float as water, yea—
i can tell you.
i have shaken rivers
out of my eyes.

off the track
i blew
and traveled with the wind
howling
there were many voices—
screammmming blooddrops of time

now, flown from the circles
and sound
there is only one tone mine
but i have lost hearing
to the wind, many voices,
and cannot remember
where to listen.

II

a silence is re-flowing
the peace that roars
inner beauty
the beat of your pulse
is lost in the
howling of the wind,
i am returning—
cradling creation in the
silences.

and i shall
travel with the wind
no more.

who wobbles through the
breeze like a chiffon palm leaf
wreathing around a bamboo
lamp post

who dropped me like a rain tear
and rubbed me all over the grass

       (i felt the bubbles bristling on my back)

who shows me how to wiggle-weave my thread (silky
through fires   cool)
as yet unsinged.

8.68

JESUS WAS CRUCIFIED, or

It Must Be Deep
(an epic pome)

i was sick
and my motha called me
tonight yeah, she did she
sd she was sorri
i was sick, but what
  she wanted tuh tell
me was that i shud pray or
have her (hunky) preacher
pray for me. she sd. i
had too much hate in me
she sd u know the way yuh think is
got a lots to do
wid the way u feel, and i
agreed, told her i WAS angry a lot THESE days
and maybe my insides was too and she sd
    why it's somethin wrong wid yo mind girl
that's what it is
            and i sd yes, i was aware a lot
lately and she sd if she had evah known educashun
woulda mad me crazi, she woulda neva sent me to
school (college that is)
she sd the way i worked my fingers to the bone in
this white mans factori to make u a de-cent some-
bodi and here u are actin not like decent folks
    talking bout hatin white folks & revolution
& such and runnin round wid NegroEs
   WHO CURSE IN PUBLIC!!!! (she sd)
THEY COMMUNIST GIRL!!! DON'T YUH KNOW THAT???
   DON'T YUH READ*THE NEWSPAPERS?????

(and i sd)

i don't believe—(and she sd) U DON'T BELIEVE IN GOD
NO MO DO U?????

u wudn't raised that way! U gon die and go tuh HELL
and i sd i hoped it wudn't be NO HUNKIES there
and she sd
what do u mean, there is some good white people and some
bad ones, just like there is negroes
and i says i had neva seen ONE (wite good that is) but
she sd negroes ain't readi, i knows this and
deep in yo heart you do too and i sd yes u right
negroes ain't readi and she sd
why just the utha day i was in the store and there was
uh negro packin clerk put uh colored woman's ice cream
in her grocery bag widout wun of them "don't melt" bags
    and the colored ladi sd to the colored clerk
"how do u know mah ice cream ain't gon tuh melt befo I
git home."
        clerk sd. "i don't" and took the ice cream
        back out and put it in wun of them "stay hard"
        bags,
and me and that ladi sd see see, ne-groes don't treat
nobody right why that clerk packin groceries was un
grown main, acted mad. white folks wudn't treat yuh that
way. why when i went tuh the BANK the otha day to de-
posit some MONEY
this white man helped me fast and nice. u gon die girl
and go tuh hell if yuh hate white folks. i sd, me and
my friends could dig it . . . hell, that is
she sd du u pray? i sd sorta when i hear Coltrane and
she sd if yuh read yuh bible it'll show u read genesis
revelation and she couldn't remember the otha chapter
i should read but she sd what was in the Bible was
happnin now, fire & all and she sd just cause i didn't
    believe the bible don't make it not true

                          (and i sd)
      just cause she believe the bible didn't make it true
and she sd it is it is and deep deep down
in yo heart u know it's true

                       (and i sd)

it must be d

                eeeep
she sd i mon pray fuh u tuh be saved. i sd thank yuh.
   but befo she hung up my motha sd
   well girl, if yuh need me call me
i hope we don't have to straighten the truth out no mo.
i sd i hoped we didn't too
              (it was 10 P.M. when she called)
she sd, i got tuh go so i can git up early tomorrow
and go tuh the social security board to clarify my
record cause i need my money.
work hard for 30 yrs. and they don't want tuh give me
$28.00 once every two weeks.
          i sd yeah . . .
don't let em nail u wid no technicalities
          git yo checks . . . (then i sd)

      catch yuh later on jesus, i mean motha!

          it must be

                deeeeep. . . .

IT IS DEEP

(don't never forget the bridge
that you crossed over on)

Having tried to use the
witch cord
that erases the stretch of
thirty-three blocks
and tuning in the voice which
   woodenly stated that the
   talk box was "disconnected"

My mother, religiously girdled in
her god, slipped on some love, and
laid on my bell like a truck,
blew through my door warm wind from the south
concern making her gruff and tight-lipped
      and scared
that her "baby" was starving.
she, having learned, that disconnection results from
          non-payment of bill (s).

She did not
recognize the poster of the
grand le-roi (al) cat on the wall
had never even seen the books of
Black poems that I have written
thinks that I am under the influence of
      communists
when I talk about Black as anything
other than something ugly to kill it befo it grows
   in any impression she would not be
considered "relevant" or "Black"
              but

there she was, standing in my room
not loudly condemning that day and
not remembering that I grew hearing her
curse the factory where she "cut uh slave"
and the cheap j-boss wouldn't allow a union,
not remembering that I heard the tears when
they told her a high school diploma was not enough,
and here now, not able to understand, what she had
been forced to deny, still—

she pushed into my kitchen so
she could open my refrigerator to see
what I had to eat, and pressed fifty
bills in my hand saying "pay the talk bill and buy
some food; you got folks who care about you. . . ."

My mother, religious-negro, proud of
having waded through a storm, is very obviously,
a sturdy Black bridge that I
crossed over, on.

Some Body Call

(for help)

i remember the night
he beat
her
we all heard her scream
him break some glass
her beg
dont do it
the hit
imagined the cut
heard the door open
her running running running
in the hall   way
screaming blood blood
saw bloods
(in my head
would not open my door
the po-lees came   (some   body   called)
say who cut de lady
in de mouth who put her out
wid no coat no shoes

        (some   body called
        some   body called

                for help)

heard the pigs take her take him a way
beat him, he beat her, beat him down the stairs
heard him call
        (for help)

no body opened no door.

next morning
there was
this blood
on the walls
see
little smudges here there
from hand from mouth (no doubt)
running running along the walls in splatters in sblobs
running running
                i could wipe the stains away
                i could do that i could
                but i thought   (surely)

                              4 weeks past)

someone (else) would have
why, the janitor
empties the garbage
mops the hall   way floors every
day but he dont touch the blood
                must be because he dont
                hear her screeeeeeaaammmmming
                do he dont he NEED to
                e-rase that blood runningstill   still
      on the walls the second floors the first floors all   over

Bloods

running running running
  against the walls

                BLOODS
        running running running
            in hall ways
running running running
             through they world
                CUT-TING into each other
        Some   Body   PLEASE call
                          for help

when I asked him about
                    it
he said he had to do
                    that.
had to
        knock her down, slap her,
beat her up, chastise her . . .
how else
would she know
he loved her?

she understood
it wasn't nothing serious
nothing, "personal"
    she'd get up knowing
she was going down again
she never would hold the floor
and wait out the count,
somehow
that would have been unfair,
not part
        of it. . . ,

she never even imagined
    packing her bags and
leaving him.
what you leave a good man fuh?
he paid the rent, went to work everyday
bought groceries,
occasionally.
why, where would she go?

and to who? who would
love her better? any "differently"
she knew he would never
kill her
she seldom had a bruise,
that showed . . .
just a knock here & now
a slap there & then
to ease the pain of
    BEING
together. . . .

once, I knocked on their door
and asked if I could help
They BOTH became angry at me
"Go home stupid! Don't you have any of your own business to mine?"
Sometimes when my neighbors are not
        fighting
they talk to me
They Say,
THEY LOVE EACH OTHER.

5.11.71

carlyle died last night
young
talented
musician.
struggling
tuh make it
tuh be famous
tuh be his dream self.

dealin in them herbs
sniffin smack droppin pills
more & more
              more
when fame didn't happen—

not rememberin that the
program
only allows for
one.
at
uh
time.
      and nowatimes
                perhaps
                    not
                        one.

                yeah. uh huh.
                carlyle died
                last night.

wite folks
sd it was uh
him-uh-rage

(in the head)

but
weBlacks
know
the ways of

genocide.

dark children
running in the streets
joyscreaming about a kite
dark children
clomping up and down on
half heels no heels half soled shoes
dodging chunks of glass
joyscreaming about a kite
a kite
that flies no higher than
the two story liquor store
they stream in front of

don't these children know
that kites will fly
higher
much higher
than two story liquor stores.

II

a dog dances around
these children
sure-footed fast tipping
dances, like a ballerina
on his tender toes—
the dog speaks, the dog knows
of
too much glass.

III

a man
in a deuce and a quarter
is staring daggers at me.
when i look,
i can see him through my
rear view mirror
he knows that soon i am going
to leave this space/
my motor is humming. . . .

he does not understand what
is taking me so long
why my head is bent towards
the pad in my lap
how could he know
i am
busy, writing poems
about liquor stores and dark children
with tender footed dogs and kites
and dusky proud men who sit and stare
daggers at me, while flaunting their
expensive pride,
in deuces and quarters
on 47th street.

3.8.70

The Children of Their Sin (an exorcise)

> *. . . they'll herd us into ghettoes*
> *jail us*
> *kill us slowly*
> *because we are the Attribute*
> *that haunts their dreams . . .*
> *. . . because we are the children of their Sin*
> *. . . who will atone . . . ?*
> *. . . Vengeance is mine and yours and his,*
> *says the testament of man*
> *nailed to the boulder of pain.*
>
> (from *Death, Somewhere, and Homeward Bound*
> by EZEKIEL MPHAHLELE)

and i moved and went
and sat next to
a white man
        because
the brother who
sat down beside me looked
mean and hungry, poor and damply cold.
    it was raining this day
and i had money in my pockets, lots of money
from work, work with Black people,
      poet-teaching
about how to love one Black another
    and
i had food in my belly and a warm snug coat on.

and,
the white man
i sat close to
was neatly new yorkish
antiseptically executive

        and i smothered faint memories and
            shadows and things. . . .

     2

one friday evening
when i was just twelve
mama was coming home
from the factory, purse
full of hand swollen pay
and a nigger ran by—
almost knocked her down
to the ground
snatched her purse
left mama holding on tight
to the strap, he broke the strap
mama screammmmed
      for bread
      for meat
      for milk
        moneeeeeeeey

help. help. and ran and chased him.
chased him. through. the dark gangway.
help. up. the alley. down. the. side. walksss
           help. help.   pleeeeeasehelp!

mama ran.   runrunrunrunrun.   ran.

                      for bread
                      for milk
                      for carfare for next weeks slave
                              moneeeeeey

            ranranranran
                    and then—
that nigger jumped. a fence!
            jumpedafence
                    andwasgone——

left mama. gone. mama came home
clutching the black purse strap and crying
clutching the black purse strap and crying and crying and crying
           all night long

two weeks later, maybe three, a colored lady called
said she found mama's purse and wallet and
all her cards that said who
she was
all mama's identifying cards. and numbers . . .
           near the colored lady's garbage cans.

                no money
           mean nigger jumped that fence and was gone

      3

i moved. and sat next to this white man today.
neat. clean. fattening and proper.
away from the brother
who looked hungry and mean and poor and cold.

But oh,
somewhere, deep deeeep in the e-qui-nox of my soul,
shuffling shadows   protested.

>i heard a coliseum of women
>   screamingMERCY
>in tongues, from the whips
>i saw purple bloodied babies falling like
>hail, ripped out from split thick black
>   bellies
>i saw a body gagging in the wind
>i heard some moans of pain, pleas for
>   MERCY
>SALVATION RETRIBUTION

and riding and riding above the crest of my
pain my shame, strangling me—

>was FEAR, distorting my love my BLACKNESS

>i heard my MAMA screaming screaming screaming
>   and cryyyyyyyyyyyyying
>mean NIGGER jumped that fence and gone

4

i moved and sat next to this
white man today

>away from that MEAN NIGGER WHO STOLE
>   MAMAS MONEY

i moved to sit next to this white man
the white man
WHO MADE THAT AFRICAN NIGGER BROTHER/   jump
    that fence and git gone

and the rage and burning shame of   conflict
set my teeth on ice
and strove to liquefy the
marrow in my bones.

5.5.71

let uh revolution come. uh
state of peace is not known to me
anyway
since i grew uhround in chi town
where
howlin wolf howled in the tavern on 47th st.
and muddy waters made us cry the salty nigger blues,
   where pee wee cut lonnell fuh messin wid
   his sistuh and blood baptized the street
   at least twice ev'ry week and judy got
   kicked outa grammar school fuh bein pregnant
   and died tryin to ungrow the seed
     we was all up in there and
       just living was guerilla warfare, yeah.

let uh revolution come.
couldn't be no action like what
i dun already seen.

Esther, as Lead

the newspaper told the story
it wudn't no big thang.
uh littl space for uh dumb
little black kid
it wudn't no big thang. . . .

it wudn't even the first time.
u git these kids dumb, who
write on tear up and eat up
the walls the holes the houses—
        destructive black bastards.

kids die ev'ry day, dumb
like people drink ev'ry day. dead.
yeah, the walls was flaky
and the kid took it all in
and her mind just shriveled up
like uh dried old prune.

and the woman what owned the
house. said in the newspapers
she knew it wudn't her fault
yeah, destructive littl black bastards
eatin up somebodis walls. . . .

the newspapers ran it down
it was just uh tiny space
cause it happens all the time
u git these kids, u know,
who be eating
they self to death.
1.24.69

He thinks the confusion
   is in him
and it is,
except it is not.
If he could only get a
tight grip on solid
on positive on real on this
sure way or that sure thing
he would run to it/run through it.
he does run.
he chases illusions
not admitting the film he sees
surrounding them
not admitting the clouds when he
gets up on them.
he chases the thought/the unspoken
the untutored that unfinished ah yes, dream
his mind willing and directing it all
trying vainly to teach himself
to stand firm/stand still
stand most of all
deep, lasting and true.
none of it. not so, not to be . . .
hair bumps of our youth.
we ride over the rough waves and
come to hills on dry land

there is no
camping ground
down here
    this
      is
        no
          promised
            land.
we can not make it so. . . .

16.
tell me
why he is no longer in school.
your eyes avoid mine,
your head is lazy
will not be held straight
you shrug your shoulders
he's 16.

he wanted to be an engineer
only yesterday—
his voice was soft,
i was allowed to kiss his cheek
he was proud of his school
his new Black books, his grades—

why did you let them get him

tell me we can share secrets, i am no one
only your sister.

i remember. you had dreams
big brother. you were going
to be
an accountant or a lawyer
the bus was only a step. i
understand. you lost your pace
in the wheels. i understand
though i never have never will
ah, but this sun, whose
voice broke loose only a moment ago—

how did we lose him. tell me.

how does he spend his time
is he a partner now of the streets
does he drop pills, guzzle
cheap blood/smoke gold dust.

i saw his walk change
from yours to the dip
to the swagger to the cool
speak. we can share secrets.
or we can shout our truth in the streets

tell me

how dare we lose him

A Train Ride

(for negro waiters)

Aging yellow men
with wavy hair
who were never called "Black,"
who were serving
when I was born,
bow with a pride
that flows slower now.

The curved hands
that carefully hold the
sallow paper plates
held silver rimmed china once,
and a ghost of the grace remains.

A slight stiffness—
at the neck, and waist—
a gliding of the feet,

remind us of the air
that rolled over us
and stripped them
of the glamour of wheels.

5.29.69

mama spent pennies
in uh gallon milk jug
saved pennies
fuh four babies
college educashuns

and when the babies
got bigger they would
secretly "borrow" mama's
pennies to buy candy

and pop cause mama
saved extras
fuh college educashuns
and pop and candy

was uh non-credit in bad teeth
mama pooled pennies
in uh gallon milk jug
Borden's by the way

and the babies went
to school cause mama saved
and spent and paid
fuh four babies
college educashuns
mama spent pennies
         and nickels
         and quarters
         and dollars

and one life.
mama spent her life
in uh gallon milk jug
fuh four Black babies
college educashuns.

BREAKTHROUGH

I've had tangled feelings lately
    about ev'rything
bout writing poetry, and otha forms
about talkin and dreamin with a
special man (who says he needs me)
      uh huh
and my mouth has been open
      most of the time, but
I ain't been saying nothin but
      thinking about ev'rything
and the partial pain has been
how do I put my self on paper
the way I want to be or am and be
not like any one else in this
Black world but me

how do I sing some lyrics ev'ry most could dig but
don't always be riffin like twenty-ten othas

      ev'rybodi's faintly heard, the trouble
is I tell you, how can I
sound just like and only my self
      and then could you dig it if I could?

u see, the changes are so many
there are several of me and
      all of us fight to show up at the same time

and there is uh consistent incongruity
    do u for instance, understand
    what I mean when I say
              I am very tired of trying

and want Blackness which is my life, want this to be
easier on me, want it not to suck me in and
out so much leavin me a balloon with no air, want it
not to puff me up so much sometimes
that I git puffed up and sucked in in to the
raunchy kind of love Black orgy I go through. do
u dig what I mean when I say I want to scream forget
it all some days and then want to cry when
I walk around the street with my hurt my mind
and some miscellaneous littl brotha
who's ultimately playin with my feelins sayin

     "what's happenin beautiful Black sistuh?"
can u dig why I want to say to him

     "why should u care?" and "why would u make me
love and puff all over again" and instead i end up
smiling and sayin, "U got it littl bro"
        because
I think he needs, and he thought I needed
                        and the
be cause is the why, and that kinda style goes on
and I become trite in my dreams
and my poems fidget and why should I care that I
can't sound as original as I think my thoughts are,
but can you dig how it could
make me question my thoughts?

     how did I ever get in this mess—
     is mess this, don't u ever sit around and want
     to get very high offa somethin and cry be cause
      u   are
and then what am I supposed to tell my self
when I want to take long bus rides and cop sunsets
for the soul I'm not sure I have/would want it, and
sometimes I want to hibernate in the summer
     and hang out in the winter and nurse babies
and get fat and lay around and be pinched by my man
and just love and laugh all the time, even if the

sun don't shine
                    and then the kids go to marching and
singing songs talkin bout Blackness and schools that
ain't schools and I know what they be talkin bout
     they know that I know what needs doin and what
has all or any of this or that got to do with the
fact that I want to write a POEM, a poem poem, a
     poem's poem poem on a poem that ev'ry u could
dig, just if only a littl bit
in between, underneath, on top or a-round a word
or feelin
          and not mind the fact that it might
sound faintly like some riffin u heard.
or not mind that it's not like anything
u could have been told about to understand
     but like reading breathing or sipp-savorin uh mind
an uh hung over ecstasy in what is and ain't gon be
and uh stiff won't rub off don't washout longing
     for what u never had and can't imagine how u could
long for it since u'r not even sure it is
anyhow, like u or I is and I really hope that
     if u read this u
     will dig where I'm at
     and feel what i mean/that/where
          i am
     and could very possibly
          be
          real
   at this lopsided crystal sweet moment. . . .

a man, standing in the shadows of a
white marble building
chipping at the stones earnestly, tirelessly,
moving with the changes of the hours,
the days,
the seasons and years,
using the shadows to shield him
such a man,
can go un noticed. . . .

a Black Man standing in the shadows
is not like the one who straggles
through open spaces, hurls bricks at
windows, shatters glass,
yanks or kicks the doors down and
beats his chest scream/proclaiming his glory—
these ones are removed, swiftly.

but the man who grows inside the shadows,
chipping at the foundation, long after
windows and door have been replaced,
the man, who becomes the dark shadow of a
white marble building, will
pick the foundation to pieces,
chip by chip, and
        the
        building
        will
        fall.

to Gwen

mo luv

    if i were a painter
        it would be easier
i suppose
        though paint i know
has its limitations.
                    how do you paint
        the pulse
            or mix the essence of
                the tender heart
        what color is love, throbbing
        through the black veins.

    if i were a musician,
            perhaps
    i
        could write a score
            with notes
        and special combinations
        advanced sounds, beyond directions
        or, you could hear
    a voice ringing around the air
        heavy, vibrato with encouragement
jazz timing at the throat
                        or i could beat drums
        and you would hear
                        but
        what is the beat of care,
        how rolls the rhythm of tender

if i were a painter
if i were a musician
    i could
    maybe, but
being the poet
                only
and knowing that luv
has its way of choking around the mind
which is somehow connected to
    these fingers
that make sounds on paper and because
the sounds are not the words and the words are not
    who you are
and description is afterall useless if i can not
    de tail you Black woman
    you our Sister
    you who i call a lady
you are the song that Billie
    was born into singing
you are the picture that Black
    people go on painting
true, you are love & lovelier & lovingest
    all that we must be and are yet to become
you are
    mo luv and mo luv and mo luv and mo luv and mo luvvvvvv

No Such Thing As A Witch/
Just A Woman, Needing Some Love

there you were,
sitting across the room
frowning at me,
and me,
raving and carrying on
like a fool.
i felt like one too.
a woman can ACT mighty witchy
when all she needs and wants, is for
   her man
to tell her to shut up!
     and then take her in
his arms,
        and deal with her.

2.11.70

(*for mama and daddy*)

my daddy don't know
the same lady
i do. i know mama
he knows "suga."
                and when daddy looks at mama
                i wonder does he see
                the wrinkles around
                the tight mouth, stiff
                factory used fingers
                uh yellow skin,
                begun to fade. . . .

and when mama talks
how does he hear? i hear
anger, pride, strength and love
crouched low in the throat,
any, ready to spring.
                but daddy calls mama "suga"
                and uh beacon is behind his eyes,
                he buys Chanel and coats
                with fur collars. . . .

i wonder what lady does daddy know?

he would fly away
his dreams would carry him
into lands where tongues
are low and soft and slow   (dope)

where nobody deigns to do
the dares
cause everybody's hip
and everybody cares. . . .

he would fly a way
   were it not for
              the woman
                   holding him
                   holding him
                   holding him with her scalloped eyes

                   holding him
                   with her leafy tongue

      yes,
         holding him, wooing him
                          stay
      holding him up,
      by
      holding him down
      his -anguish- down
             as he watches his dreams
                 tremble
                     and fall
         like autumn leaves to the ground.

I

i heard you today
when you breezed by
me, glanced at my face
and didn't drop a
sound, i heard you
in spite of what the
soundmasters say. and

i just want you to know that
if it weren't for my
genie (who by the way is Jealous of you),
transforming my feet into feathers
and melting a steel plate onto
the top of my tongue,

i would have cooed you back or
trickled you down.

II

i kept feeling all over my world for you
and you weren't there. except that you
were/are, but why at the end of my dreams
          (they don't stop right when you butt in)
or in the pause of every significant speech
i try to make. who told you you could
bee (at least in my thing anyhow) i
mean don't you think you're being
very silly using up precious time

when you could be doing something
really! important and here you are
tying up my mind in skinny little
knots and balancing them on the tip
of my tongue.

III

i've told myself
a hundred times that
it don't make sense
to think all these
love poems to someone
who ain't here/there or   close/far a-round   Therefore:
i've decided today (i've decided a lot of things lately)
i'll stop believing in dreams   that
in fact, just as soon as i
finish writing my last poem

For Some Black Men

A woman finds it hard
to/give for/give, a man
whose calling card's
a hardness.
Woman is softness,
warm of warmth
need from need.

Woman is child,
holds a hurt or lip up to be kissed.
Man's stand is show and tell
adjust or fix,
tall to small
stiffness comes
later.
Pieces fit. People flow
   together

Poem for Some Black Women

i am lonely.
all the people i know
i know too well

there was comfort in that
at first but now
we know each others miseries
        too well.
we are
    lonely women, who spend time waiting for
        occasional flings

we live with fear.
we are lonely.
we are talented, dedicated, well read
        BLACK, COMMITTED,

we are   lonely.

we understand the world problems
Black women's problems with Black men
        but all
we really understand is
        lonely.

when we laugh,
we are so happy to laugh
we cry when we laugh
    we are lonely.
we are busy people
always doing things

fearing getting trapped in rooms
loud with empty . . .
                    yet
knowing the music of silence/hating it/hoarding it
loving it/treasuring it,
   it often birthing our creativity
              we   are   lonely

being soft and being hard
supporting our selves, earning our own bread
soft/hard/hard/soft/
knowing that need must not show
                              will frighten away
knowing that we must
walk back-wards nonchalantly on our tip-toesssss
   into
happiness,
   if only for stingy moments

we know too much
we learn to understand everything,
to make too much sense out
of the world,
of pain
      of lonely . . .

we buy clothes, we take trips,
we wish, we pray, we meditate, we curse, we crave, we coo, we caw,

      we need ourselves sick, we need, we need
we lonely we grow tired of tears we grow tired of fear
we grow tired but must al-ways be soft and not too serious . . .
   not too smart not too bitchy not too sapphire
   not too dumb not too not too not too
a little less a little more
                    add here detract there

                    .lonely.

I Have Been Hungry

Preface: This poem was written because I was asked to contribute to
an anthology of black and white women, and the title of the
anthology was *I Had Been Hungry All My Years*.

I

and you white girl
shall i call you sister now?
can we share any secrets of sameness,
any singularity of goals. . . .
you, white girl with the head that
perpetually tosses over-rated curls
while i religiously toss my over-rated behind
you white girl
i am yet suspicious of/
for deep inside of me
there is the still belief that
i am
a road
you would travel
to my man.

2

and how could you, any of you
think that a few loud words and years
could erase the tears
blot out the nightmares and knowledge,
smother the breeded mistrust

49

and how could any of you think that i
after being empty for so long
could fill up on fancy fierce platitudes. . . .

    some new/old knowledge has risen in me like yeast
     but still old doubts deflate

am i—really—so beautiful
as i sweat and am black and oh so
greasy in the noonday sun

the most beauty that i am i am inside
and so few deign to touch
i am a forest of expectation.
the beauty that i will be is yet
to be defined

    what i can be even i can not know.

3

    and what does a woman want?
what does any woman want
but a soft man to hold her hard
a sensitive man to help her fight off
the insensitive pangs of living.
and what is living to a woman
without the weight of some man
pulling her down/puffing her out

    do not tell me
liberated tales of woman/woeman
who seek only to satisfy them selves
with them selves, all, by them selves

i will not believe you
i will call you a dry canyon
them, a wilderness
of wearying and failures
a fearing of hungerings from
and deep into
the wonderment of loneliness
and what makes any woman so.

4

as for me—
i am simple
a simple foolish woman.
all that i have ever wanted
i have not had
and much of what i have had
i have not wanted.

   my father never wanted three girls
and only one son, one sun. . . .
God, how he wished his seeds
had transformed themselves into
three boys and only one girl—
for heaven's sake, only one good for nothing
wanting needing love and approval seeking bleeding
girl.
and so, i have spent my days
so many of my days seeking the approval
which was never there
craving the love
i never got
and what am i now,
no longer a simple girl
bringing lemonade and cookies
begging favor

and what am i now
no longer a world-torn woman
showering my "luck" in a
cold bottle of cold duck

and—who—am i now
but a
saved
sighing
singular thing. a woman. . . .
ah, here i am
and
here have i been
i say,
i
have been hungry,
ravenously hungry,
all
my
years

the fact is
that i don't hate any body any more
  i went through my mean period
  if you remember i spit out nails
   chewed tobacco on the paper
and dipped some bad snuff.
   but in one year
just like i woke up one morning and
  saw my mother's head gray
and i asked myself/could it have turned
    overnight?
knowing full well the grayness had been
  coming and had even been there
   awhile
just like that i woke up one morning
 and looked at my self
  and what i saw was
      carolyn
  not imani ma jua or soul sister poetess of
    the moment
  i saw more than a "sister" . . .
   i saw a Woman. human.
       and black.
   i felt a spiritual transformation
    a root revival of love
   and i knew that many things
    were over
  and some me of—beauty—
       was about to begin. . . .

you think you
need me. think
that i
will complete some picture for you.
total up and be the sum
of something, your thing . . .
but it's a lie you know
you've almost come up on
the truth about yourself
and you want me to hold
you/hold the truth off
when the pain comes
of lying too much.
when the awkward moments
descend from closing ones eyes too often
you want me to present my self
for the wrapping.
you want to wrap your self
up in me/   i in you and we
will hide behind each other
and that will be the only
truth between us.
we, us ducking and hiding and
running and blinding ourselves.

II

i could help you.
i could become the vital
part of your struggle

whenever the truth comes
too near
i could divert you
with my body at first,
perhaps later with marriage and
a child
something to weigh you
or divert your attention.
you know how women do.
i could find some thing
that would be sufficient
and then you would be able
to smile.

III

and of course
you promise to do
the same for me.
you promise to lie to me
about me to me to others. . . .
we promise to present a
united front to our friends
to the world.
we promise not to expose
but to preserve each other's
weaknesses.
i will forgive
and we will both
forget

gracefully . . .
except of course at
the times when we must
most painfully remind each other
of the function we are
                    performing
for each other less one of us
forgets one day
and steps one step too far from
our masquerade.

we could be together only
if i promised to keep my mouth
shut and speak on cue.
you propose to pay me with
the hard and softness of your body.
that is what you bait me with.
your soft mouth and your unconsciously
deceitful face.

it is not enough for me.
it is not enough for you.
together we must plunge
deeper into our pain for more—
for the more pain we attempt to escape
the more joy we automatically negate
for it is through pain that we
ultimately realize the specific beautiful or ugly
innards of
our
selves.

Food for Thought

you understand how
very often
you are
the one
who creates the traps
you fall into.

              the thing that destroys a person/a people
            is not the knowing
               but the knowing and not
                      doing.

strange
    how we women
   know
     when a man
     leaves us—
     even when
     he's still
     with us. . . .

  when you need
    give

it is not ugly to dream in life
   but it is ugly to make life a dream

      i wonder if
      the sunrays are like the fingertips of
        God?

The wind blew my father from the south to the north.
He came with a heart as deep and as wide as a tunnel—
he came with a dream and a hope for a beautiful harmonious future.
He came, Daddy was a prayer, a jitterbug hymn and a collard/
cornbread sweet potato/green country psalm. . . .

> the city sifted him like wheat from chaff
> like corn from husks, and the wind that blew
> him here blew him down, blew him around, while
> the flashing lights glazed his eyes and rechanneled
> his heart in a new direction. He became a new dimension.

He learned how to lock and close doors and bar windows. He
bought dogs not for love, but for protection. He learned to
carry guns not for harmless hunting but for restraining men.
He learned how to be cool, not country, to be stiff and serious and
silent. Laughter was reserved for home and homebodies, home folk.
He was a tree, with cautious and displaced roots, walking the streets
with feet that hurt, with feet too big for computerized shoes that
tapped the rhythm of concrete, and not the loving crush of green
grass.

2

> every since my father been
>   here wid me
> his feets has hurt him
> they been tired and flat wid a crop of corns
>   feet kept daddy out of the wars
> and he was glad
>   when he went for his examination
> he say the white man told him everything was wrong wid
>   his feet

they was in such bad shape.
my daddy say he told the white man "ain't nothin wrong
wid my feets, except they 'smart' a lot
they was born hurting and tired and flat.
cause they knows so much history. . . ."
The history, the root, the strength of my father is the strength we
now rest on.

Like rocks, our fathers and their brothers came and sweated
in factories, prowled the streets for day labor and pennies for their
expensive blood. They stayed with their children or pawned them
out to loving Big Mamas or Big Daddys and their card-playing
and drinking was their balm in an evil Gilead. They had a sense of
a portion of honor in them, their God was their strength, their
pride, their purpose, their faith. . . .

And no one had to tell them they were Black/they graced their
mirrors every morning . . .   and did what they could
to retain some love, some dignity, some honor, while they lost
their sons to wild city streets and wars, their women to white men's
kitchens and corners.

They gave to us a portion of their grace, they gave to us
a legacy of hope, they pushed us out, us kicking and screaming,
through rapacious schools, hoping that somehow an education
for us would right the wrongs for them.

And we grew loud and bold and stupidly brave and taught
ourselves with Marx and Mills to call them weak and useless, as the
holocaust of the sixties began.
We blamed them for surviving, we blamed them for living as
best they
could, we blamed them for what history did not allow
them
or even us to do—never remembering that the
love
we had for ourselves was the love they gave us.

When I was a child my father was the fix-it man
everything that went wrong in our house my father could fix
I thought my father could fix everything.

      I grew and learned sorrow. . . .
   I had a puppy, and because we had rats in our house
      my mother laid poisoning on our bare part dirt-part
   linoleum floors. And my puppy, being animal, being curious,
      being stupid, ate the poison and died.
Was the poison really for the rat, was it for the dog, or was it
      for us . . . the Black niggers caught in the dirty
        misery constrained ghetto?
   The puppy died; and mama tried to throw him out.
But I was a child, a child who believed in daddy, big Black daddy,
      the fix-it man, and I would not let mama throw my puppy
      away
   because I *believed that when my daddy came home*
      from work he could fix that dead dog.
I was a child, a Black child who believed in a Black man.
      the sixties stripped us of such a love and trust.
  and we ran naked in the streets, changing our hair, our food,
our God, our dress, condemning our elders and screaming obscenities
      at each other and others—in the name of "revolution," in
the name of positive change.
      we stripped ourselves of our heritage, of tradition,
of the strength of old wise men who were our cushions of love,
      who gave us extravagant care, who were our rocks
in this weary land.

4

Now, I am no longer a child, I have tasted sorrow.

only, in these last few hours, these last immutable days,
I have seen my father's son, my brother, shot down in the night
by Blackmen, wearing naturals no doubt, Blackmen molded in
the model of Shaft.
And I have seen my father's heart, that funnel of love turn into a
sieve of dust. . . .
And at my brother's graveside I watched my father, your father,
all our fathers sit, stiff and strong, brave and proud and
ramrodded in grief, I saw our sons and brothers. . . .
I saw the Jesus in my father's hands, saw the wino in his
feet turned out like shuffle, saw the doctor, lawyer, preacher
in his face, saw the construction worker in his back,
saw his actual hair turn white and gray, saw him fold into
himself his body limp like some autumn leaf opening
and closing in the beating rain I saw him and all our fathers
and knew. We must look at our old men, look to them
for strength, for knowledge, for direction and learn what they have
always known. That love and *respect is our*
beginning. Love and respect is our end. We must learn how
to love, to protect, to cherish, our young, our old, our
own.

mama's God never was no white man.
her My Jesus, Sweet Jesus never was neither.
the color they had was the color of
her aches and trials, the tribulations of her heart
mama never had no saviour that would turn
his back on her because she was black
when mama prayed, she knew who she
was praying to and who she was praying to
didn't and ain't got
no color.

Jesus must of been some kind of dude

(for James and Esther Mitchell and family)

Jesus must of been
some kind of dude
even though they crucified
him
I think he whipped game on em
though
cause he strutted on up and out
again
   after three days
   one day for resting
   one day for mourning
   and one day for just getting on up

Yeah, he must of been some kind
of dude, I'm telling you
he must a been a real mean actor
walking on top of the water
feeding thousands of folks with
five loaves of bread and two little fishes
raising folks up from the dead
changing water to wine
making the dumb to talk and the blind to see

Jesus was a militant dude sisters.
A revolutionary cat brothers,
a whole lot of members saw and touched him
he was sho'nuff fuh real but remember ole
doubting Thomas who had to stick his finger in
Jesus' side before he would believe?

And Jesus had a boss black natural too
they say it was natural like lambs wool
and feet—like burnt brass

And remember when Peter and all the others was in that
ship and the wind and water was cutting up cutting em
down and they saw somebody walking on the water
       Peter thought it was a vision
       He say I gots to be seeing things now,
who done spiked the holy wine?
  How this dude Jesus gon walk on
         some WATER!

But Jesus was cool and his rap was heavy, he just pulled
    Peter on
         out and don't you know
       Peter walked out on the water too!

Wow. they was some
             badddd dudes. . . .

And Black men say sister loves what do you want us to do
      how you want us to be
And we say be like medgar
            a love rock like Jesus
    be like martin
          a love rock like Jesus
    be like malcolm was be-coming
               a love rock
                  like Jesus

Jesus keep coming, knocking at our doors
and we don't even recognize him when we see him.

Stand up brothers and sisters and let Jesus come into
      yo heart.

and when the revolution came

(for Rayfield and Lillie and the whole rest)

and when the revolution came
the militants said
niggers wake up
you got to comb yo hair
the natural way
        and the church folks say oh yeah?   sho 'nuff . . .
and they just kept on going to church
gittin on they knees and praying
and tithing and building and buying

and when the revolution came
the militants said
niggers you got to change
the way you dress
and the church folk say oh yeah?
        and they just kept on going to church
with they knit suits and flowery bonnets
and gittin on they knees and praying
and tithing and building and buying

and when the revolution came
the militants said
you got to give up
white folks and the
        church folk say oh yeah? well?
never missed what we never had
and they jest kept on going to church
with they nice dresses and suits and
praying and building and buying

and when the revolution came
the militants say you got to give up
pork and eat only brown rice and
health food and the
                              church folks said uh hummmm
and they just kept on eating they chitterlings and
going to church and praying and tithing and
building and buying

and when the revolution came
the militants said
all you church going niggers
got to give up easter and christmas
and the bible
cause that's the white man's religion
and the church folks said well well well well well

and then the militants said we got to
build black institutions where our children
call each other sister and brother
and can grow beautiful, black and strong and grow in black grace
and the church folks said yes, lord Jesus we been calling each other
sister and brother a long time

and the militants looked around
after a while and said hey, look at all
these fine buildings we got scattered throughout
the black communities some of em built wid schools and nurseries
who do they belong to?

and the church folks said, yeah.
we been waiting fo you militants
to realize that the church is an eternal rock

now why don't you militants jest come on in
we been waiting for you
we can show you how to build
    anything that needs building
and while we're on our knees, at that.

sometimes
    it is painful
        you know
  to be able to see
        what people frantically try to hide
            to hear—exactly—what people are
                saying
                    and not saying. . . .
            i do get tired of tuning in
            and hearing and seeing
                when i'm tired
                    when i'm sick and tired
                        and still . . .
                            to be able to stand off
                            and see even my self
                                here or there,
                        like some
                                flower or tree
                        to see my self as the sun or river or road
                                to see myself as one of the forevers. . . .
        oh, to be a piece fitter
      to see the puzzle
    and watch my own mind
                                    always
fitting pieces together
so as to stand back and look
  at the picture
the many people
the joining and merging and breaking
    no doubt
it is divine. a gift.

and has got plenty to do
   with
          blessings. . . .
do you suppose Jesus
                    ever
       felt
          my way?

Love—The Beginning and The End

(intra means within)

the first aspect is love
is the Black Man and Black Woman
intragether.

   We have not yet learned to
hear, each other's inner voices, nor
move, within the rhythm of each other's pulses
  had not yet
cared to understand the gropings of
 one to the other. . . .

Black Man
  move into a Woman
  rush into her
scatter your seeds, plant your dreams
in her
  and you
   Black Woman
      open open
your self, open & bare your
softest fear, your nakedest secret
 open open to flow

intras-twos into ones to hundreds to thousands
open Black Woman, open Black Man

W

O

M A N

A

N

the last aspect is Love.

(women are the fruit of the earth)

AMAZING GRACE

he does not know
he is the song that she is
        singing. . . .
she goes to church
    alone
sadly every Sunday
    alone
longing for his presence
to warm her sides
longing for his lips
to join with hers
    in praise

every Sunday
she sits
on the mourners' bench*
  for him
clapping her hands
    glory in her
raining tears
  till her singing is a shout, a dance and a
        hallelujah!
as she glimpses the growth
    her suffering serves
she is filled with a glory within

* mourners' bench—a specified section of the church where people sit who seek
to meet the Lord. Some saved people go and sit "in proxy" for their unsaved
loved ones.

when she returns home
drained and so peace filled
he berates her little Bible
bombards her with questions of
the why's of suffering and sin
wars and disease and long lonely agonizing deaths.
questions
she can only partially attempt to answer.
and so, he tries to blow her mind with the wild wind
of his own fear
of her and her *holiness*
Foul names he calls her
for he is afraid
that he is no longer the
first love of her life—
and he is right.

2

she loves him,
as she loves life.
she is natural. a woman—
who clings to his tender & sweet touch.

she is mostly silent taking his abuses
when she can.
as he cuts her with words that
wisely know her
human weaknesses.

she is mostly silent
taking it all in
her heart
heavy, half broken
bowed and weight-filled
in the balance and scale of her things.

He does not know he saps a strength from her.
   a strength she has been filled with
      and freely given to her
   she hopes that one day he will
  come to know the Master whom she serves.

   and so, from week to week,
 she goes to church
     alone
  shouting and moaning
praising, singing and praying
  while he continues
     from
         week to week
     never knowing
     that from hour to hour
         day to day
he is alive
somewhat saved
somehow sanctified

because of the song she is singing
    goes on singing
       even when she is not in church
       even when she has no Bible
       even when she cries in pain

3

even when he stomps out the
door leaving her for a
   shot of whiskey
      or a game of pool or a round of cards with the boys
         she goes on
                singing
                   singing
                      singing
                         amazing
                            grace. . . .

seasons/changes moods
the things of this earth
are the things that give us pleasure.
the sunset and glow, the rise . . .
the grass blue or green, thin or tall
yet growing
the common flowers or special
the sky blue or gray smiling or sad
the air warm or wet, cold wind and wild
or sweet and careful to the feel,
a loving
touch.
these seasons are the things we love
the rhythm that keeps us moving
together or alone we take it or share it—
the things of this earth
are the things that give us pleasure.

how i got ovah II/ It Is Deep II

(for Evangelist Richard D. Henton)

just when i thought i had gotten away
my mother
called me on the phone
and did not ask,
but commanded me
to come to church with her.

and because i knew so much
and had "escaped"
i thought it a harmless enough act.

i was not prepared for the Holy Ghost.
i was not prepared to be covered by the
blood of Jesus.

i was not ready to be dipped in
                              the water. . . .

i could not drink the water turned wine.

and so i went back another day
trying to understand the mysteries
of mystical life the "intellectual"
purity of mystical light.
and that Sunday evening while i was
sitting there and the holy gospel choir
was singing
        "oh oh oh oh somebody touched me"

somebody touched me.
                          and when i turned around to
see what it was whoever touched me wanted
my mother leaned over and whispered in my ear
          "musta been the hand of the Lord"

come now, don't be afraid
i only want to run in you like blood
    a line
  draw this between us
only come and listen to my song
    a strong yet fragile blackbird

i can make music
if you will, i tell you
i can be the very thing or thought
you can not quite spit out.

    here we are
in this old western house
running together like water
tasting each other and spitting each other out
like we are so much bitter wind or wine.

    there is no way to find your selves, except this
      accept this,
    plunge in life and deep at that
and then swim until you reach some
momentary imaginary shore
    it will be God running through you
your fingers, the wet that you shake from
your head and mouth and mind
it will be God running through you
    running you through . . .
knowing no proper direction,
knowing no limited course.

II

   i have no dream but
to walk and tell you what i am told.
   there are things that happen to me
by perception or time
i am whispered to, late at night
     early morning
words pass through me
words rearrange them selves in my head
they pass through me like wild wind or fire
      winding its way around you/me
pushing me along any street that is not mine
     or your own.
here we are in the midst of hell
     and i dream of words that will
smack you all together into heaven.

III

     i have been quiet so long
it is a familiar fear
i keep feeling my mouth with my tongue
  afraid that something has slipped loose
  dropped out all the time i was opening and closing
  saying nothing nothing nothing
  i keep expecting to find some evidence that
  my private well is dry
  i am getting a warm wet
  even if i am screaming for a flood.

  could i tell you about any of
  the things that i have heard
  recently or seen
  is there such a well of a way
  still in me?

to bring you across the bridge our
blood and bones create
if i think too hard,
if i think too long
i will tell you only of pain
and fear
and envy and greed
    and cancerous rampant loneliness
and i fear you will take my laughs of joy
my tears of pain, of sorrow,
as stray whinings of western winds.

IV

there IS a well in me
    if i open up i can
        flow forever
i am surely a shout that can
    shimmy right on up to heaven
            i think sometimes
                when i write
            God has his hand on me
        i am his little black slim ink pen.